To:

_____

From:

_____

Date:

_____

GOOD NIGHT,
My Darling Dear

Prayers and Blessings
for You

Amy Kavelaris

Tommy
NELSON

An Imprint of Thomas Nelson

Good Night, My Darling Dear

© 2020 by Amy Kavelaris

Published in Nashville, Tennessee, by Tommy Nelson. Tommy Nelson is an imprint of Thomas Nelson. Thomas Nelson is a registered trademark of HarperCollins Christian Publishing, Inc.

Tommy Nelson titles may be purchased in bulk for educational, business, fund-raising, or sales promotional use. For information, please email SpecialMarkets@ThomasNelson.com.

Library of Congress Cataloging-in-Publication Data

Names: Kavelaris, Amy, author.
Title: Good night, my darling dear / Amy Kavelaris.
Description: Nashville, Tennessee : Tommy Nelson, [2020]
Identifiers: LCCN 2019013082 | ISBN 9781400212460 (hardcover)
Subjects: LCSH: Parent and child--Religious
 aspects--Christianity--Miscellanea. | Children--Prayers and devotions.
Classification: LCC BV4529 .K38 2020 | DDC 242/.62--dc23
LC record available at https://lccn.loc.gov/2019013082
ISBN 978-1-4002-1246-0

Printed in Italy
23   RTLO   8

Mfr: RTLO / Milan, Italy / July 2023 / PO # 12206990

For
My sunshine, rainbow, and starlight:
Millie, *Lou*, and *Ana Bloom*
May you shine bright, reflecting your maker

MATTHEW 5:14–16

My heart is full, my darling dear.
You're a *dream come true*.
The moment when your life began,
A part of mine did too.

As you drew your newborn breath,

Light danced upon your cheek.

Your soul sang of *adventure*

Though your mouth could not yet speak.

So as you fall asleep, sweet child,
Upon your cozy bed,
Let's dream *big dreams* for what's to come—
The journey that's ahead.

You'll leave your mark around the globe
With every chance you take.
But most of all, I'm proudest of
The *difference* that you'll make.

It's your gift to spread God's light
Wherever you may be.
When people need a *blink of hope*,
Then you're the light they'll see.

Don't hold back, my darling dear.
Be *bold*, be *brave*, be *YOU*!
God made you for amazing things
That only you can do.

Guess what? Here's a secret
Between just you and me—

Those things that fill your heart with joy
Show who you're *meant to be*.

Whatever gift you have, my love,
Applaud your friends' gifts too!
For you will *rise up tall*, dear one,
Lifting others up with you.

I wish you'd stay this little, dear,
But if it cannot be,
I'm just as keen to watch you fly,
My *starlight* by the sea.

Waltz along the ocean shore.
Grab the sunset in the sky.
Now with those vibrant hues in hand,
Paint the *canvas* of your life.

And when you see a rainbow
Shining in the sky afar,
God's painting you a picture
Of the *miracle* you are.

But now you need to rest, my dear.
Let's pray beside your bed.
Then fall asleep with all those *wondrous*
Thoughts inside your head.

As you enter into *dreamland*
And swing among the stars,
Tuck this away and keep it close—
Believe it in your heart.

You'll never be without my love.
I'll always keep you near.
But night has come; it's time to say

Good night,
my darling dear.